Milk & Cookies Press
Manhanset House
POB 342
Dering Harbor NY 11965
bricktower@aol.com ● www.ibooksinc.com

Cover design by Dean Motter
Interior design by Gilda Hannah
Edited by Howard Zimmerman
Front and back cover art by Jan Sovak

Art Credits: Pages 1, 21 © 2002 Jan Sovak. Page 3 © 2002 Joe Tucciarone.
Pages 3, 12, 25, 27 © 2002 Phil Wilson. Page 7 © 2002 D. W. Miller.
Pages 8-9 © 2002 Mark Hallett. Page 11 © 2002 Christopher Srnka.
Page 15 © 2002 Wayne Barlowe. Page 17 © 2002 Robert Walters. Pages 18 (inset), 22-23, 32 © 2002 John Sibbick.
Page 19 © 2002 Rich Penney. Pages 20, 31 © 2002 Gregory S. Paul.
Pages 29-29 © 2002 Donna Braginetz. Page 30 © 2002 Douglas Henderson.

Library of Congress Cataloging-in-Publication Data

Olshevsky, George.
Velociraptor / by George Olshevsky and Sandy Fritz.
p.cm.—(Discovering dinosaurs)
1. JUVENILE NONFICTION / Animals / Dinosaurs & Prehistoric Creatures.
2. JUVENILE NONFICTION / History / Prehistoric.
3. JUVENILE NONFICTION / Animals / Reptiles & Amphibians.

ISBN 978-1-59687-754-2

First Milk & Cookies printing, December 2025

VELOCIRAPTOR

Sandy Fritz and George Olshevsky

MILK &
COOKIES
PRESS
™

Milk & Cookies Press
Habent Sua Fata Libelli

Dinosaurs lived on Earth from about 227 million to 65 million years ago. Scientists call this the Mesozoic era. It is also called the Age of Reptiles or the Age of Dinosaurs. Dinosaurs were closely related to today's reptiles and birds. In fact, many scientists now think that birds evolved from a small meat-eating dinosaur that was a swift runner. All dinosaurs were land animals. Flying reptiles (called pterosaurs) and reptiles that swam in the sea also lived during this period, but they were not dinosaurs.

The Age of Dinosaurs, the Mesozoic era, is divided into three periods. The earliest period is called the Triassic, which lasted from 248 million to 205 million years ago. Dinosaurs first appeared around the middle of this period. The Jurassic period followed, lasting from 205 million to 145 million years ago. The final period is called the Cretaceous. The Cretaceous spanned from 145 million to 65 million years ago. After the Cretaceous, dinosaurs were gone.

But during their time, dinosaurs lived everywhere on Earth, even in Antarctica. About 700 different kinds of dinosaurs have been unearthed, and many more remain in the ground awaiting discovery. There were meat-eating dinosaurs that could run fast on their long hind legs. There were four-legged, plant-eating dinosaurs 150 feet (46 m) long and weighing as much as 100 tons (91 t)! There were dinosaurs with horns, crests, and bony armor. Some dinosaurs, both meat-eaters and plant-eaters, were as small as chickens or house cats.

Everything we know about dinosaurs comes from fossils that people have dug up from the ground. Scientists examine, measure, and analyze these fossils. From them we can learn when and where dinosaurs lived. We have learned how dinosaurs walked and ran, what they hunted, and what plants they ate. We can even figure out how long they lived. Presented in this series is the most up-to-date information we have learned about dinosaurs. We hope you'll enjoy reading all about the fabulous beasts of Earth's distant past.

Velociraptor and Its World

*V*elociraptor was a small, deadly, two-legged meat-eater that first appeared late in the Age of Dinosaurs. Measuring just six feet (2 m) long and weighing less than 100 pounds (40 kg), *Velociraptor* was about the length of a Great Dane. Half of its length was taken up by a stiff tail. It was very speedy, and had a large brain.

Some of the most unique fossils ever found record the final life-and-death struggle between a *Velociraptor* and a *Protoceratops*, an early relative of the four-legged plant-eater *Triceratops*. A sand storm hit just as the *Velociraptor* was attacking, killing both predator and prey. A taloned hand grips the frill of the *Protoceratops* and one sharp claw is sunk deep in the victim's throat. But the *Protoceratops* was defending itself; one of the *Velociraptor*'s arms is locked in the plant-eater's jaw. Both predator and prey died locked in battle. They became fossilized at the moment of death.

A full-grown *Velociraptor* catches sight of a primitive mammal. It may become the dinosaur's next meal.

Pictured here are a pair of *Deinonychus*, *Velociraptor's* larger cousin. It was about twice the length, and had a shorter snout and larger claws.

The world was a different place when *Velociraptor* roamed the earth. About 85 to 80 million years ago, during the late Cretaceous period, most of the world was warm and tropical. There was no ice at the north and south poles. Rainfall was plentiful. The warmth and the moisture caused an explosion of plant growth. There were many plant-eating dinosaurs to feed on the rich plant life. Some of these plant-eating dinosaurs, four-legged giants called sauropods, grew to be the tallest and heaviest animals ever to walk the earth. Other plant-eaters were medium sized, such as the 30-foot-long (9 m) "duck-billed" dinosaur *Parasaurolophus*, or small, such as the six-foot-long (2 m) *Protoceratops*. *Velociraptor* may have hunted them all, except for the giants. It's possible, however, that *Velociraptor* fed on the dead bodies of large plant-eaters that had died from other causes.

The Dromaeosaurid Family

Velociraptor belonged to a group of dinosaurs called the dromaeosaurids. They were a family of small to mid-sized two-legged meat-eaters. The 30-foot-long (9 m) *Utahraptor* and *Achillobatos* are the largest known dromaeosaurs. *Deinonychus* reached a length of up to 13 feet (4 m). *Velociraptor* was one of the smaller dromaeosaurids.

The dromaeosaurids hunted and killed in a way much different from other predatory dinosaurs. *Tyrannosaurus rex* and other large meat-eaters had huge skulls and jaws filled with lots of razor-sharp teeth. They killed by biting. Dromaeosaurids killed by leaping on their prey and slashing at it with their long, sharp foot claws.

Velociraptor is pictured here covered with fuzz and feathers. So far, all of the dinosaurs found with feathers have come from the same group, known as maniraptoran theropods.

Velociraptor and the other dromaeosaurids were swift animals. They ran on their hind legs, leaving their long arms free. The powerful, clawed hands of dromaeosaurids could rip and tear at prey.

A dromaeosaurid's most deadly weapon might have been its brain. Dromaeosaurids had the largest brain size compared to body size of any dinosaur family. Scientists think these clever, deadly dinosaurs used their large brains to cooperate and hunt together in packs.

Velociraptor Discovered

Velociraptor packs may have roamed areas that were once ancient prairies. Most of their fossils have been found on land that was once mostly dry, with streams and creeks running through it. Their natural range probably resembled present-day Arizona and Nevada. Mongolia's Gobi Desert is the only place where *Velociraptor* fossils have been found. Here, the bare cliffs hold fossil clues about many dinosaurs that roamed this area millions of years ago.

Velociraptor was discovered in 1924, when American dinosaur hunters visited Mongolia. Studying the dinosaur, scientists could tell it was built for speed. A long, curved claw was found on each of the animal's feet.

A *Deinonychus* pack attacks a dying ankylosaur. If it were healthy, this plant-eater covered with spikes and bony armor would not be their choice for a meal.

These claws were clearly used as weapons when this meat-eater lived. And so the dinosaur was named for its two main traits. The word *Velociraptor* means "speedy hunter" in Latin.

A Predator's Tools

Many of the features of *Velociraptor* show how specialized it was for chasing and killing prey. Unlike the largest meat-eating dinosaurs, *Velociraptor* had long arms. Attached to the end of these long arms were powerful, clawed hands. The hands were far less flexible than the human hand but could still deliver killing, slashing blows.

Velociraptor ran and walked on two legs. This upright stance kept its head held high, which was important for spotting its next meal. The neck bones of *Velociraptor* line up in an S-shaped curve. This kept the dinosaur's head high as it ran, allowing it to keep sight of its prey. And *Velociraptor* was a fast animal. Scientists estimate its top speed could have been as much as 40 miles (64 km) an hour. Modern ostriches also run this fast. Not many plant-eaters were fast enough to outrun an attacking *Velociraptor*.

Velociraptor had deadly weapons on its feet. All four toes on each foot had claws. But the second toe held an enormous claw, twice as long as the others. It curved like a half-moon and ended in a sharp point. It rarely touched the ground, so it never got worn down. The claw had one special purpose. It was *Velociraptor*'s key killing weapon.

Velociraptor and its cousins are sometimes known as "raptors." In the movie *Jurassic Park*, the *Velociraptor* stars were simply called "raptors." But the creatures shown in *Jurassic Park* were a movie invention. The movie showed them far larger than they were in real life. The size of the movie raptors more closely matches *Velociraptor*'s cousin, *Deinonychus*.

Because of its large eyes and keen eyesight, scientists think *Velociraptor* may have hunted at dusk or at night.

Scientists think that dromaeosaurids attacked by leaping on their prey and making deep, slicing wounds with their killer claws. A sharp, fast kick, and the toe claws could cut open the belly of a *Velociraptor's* prey. In the much larger *Utahraptor*, the killing claw was a foot (31 cm) long. *Velociraptor's* deadly claw measured about four inches (10 cm) long.

Kicking and clawing were two ways that a *Velociraptor* could attack. It also had another weapon—its teeth. About 80 teeth crowded *Velociraptor's* long snout. The teeth had curvy edges on them like a bread knife. This made it easier for the teeth to saw through flesh and bone. Pound for pound, *Velociraptor* was among the most powerful dinosaur predators known. Only dromaeosaurids had such a deadly combination of weapons.

Predators generally rely on keen senses. *Velociraptor* was no exception. A cavity connected to its nose took up almost half of the animal's skull. This means *Velociraptor* had an amazing sense of smell. It could probably smell a potential meal from miles away.

Each of the killing claws on *Velociraptor's* feet (right) grew to about four inches (10 cm) long, while those of *Deinonychus* were about six inches (15 cm) long.

The skulls of two hatchling *Velociraptors* were found near the nest of another meat-eater, *Oviraptor*. Some scientists think the *Velociraptors* were killed by the *Oviraptor* in order to protect its nest. But the young *Velociraptors* may have been killed by the *Oviraptor* to feed to its own babies.

Velociraptors did not have eyes facing forward, as did *T. rex* and other hunting dinosaurs. Instead, their eyes faced to the side, as in birds. This gave them a broad view, but may have limited their sense of depth. When they got close to their prey, they probably attacked based on smell rather than sight.

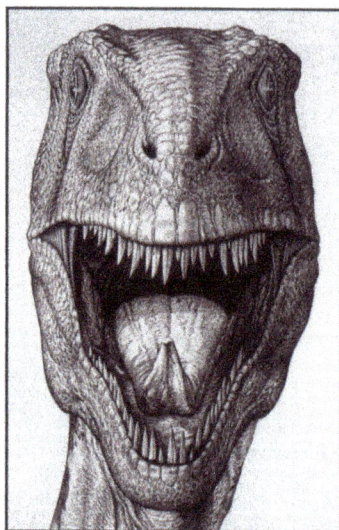

Tales the Fossils Tell

When the first dinosaur fossils were discovered, scientists thought the animals they came from were just giant reptiles. Many large reptiles, such as crocodiles and alligators, drag their tails on the ground, so scientists assumed that dinosaurs were also tail-draggers. But the trackways of dinosaurs' fossilized footprints tell a different story. When an alligator walks through a muddy or sandy patch, it leaves three sets of tracks. One set is the footprints made by the left feet. Another is the footprints made by the right feet. And the third track is a groove between the feet. This groove is made by the tail as it drags along behind the reptile. Dinosaurs left only two sets of tracks—left and right footprints. There were no grooves between them made by a tail dragging on the ground. This shows that

A pack of dromaeosaurs attacks a young ceratopsian. The sharp horns can be dangerous, but if the pack is large enough it will kill the plant-eater.

This page: The skeleton
of *Velociraptor* shows
how many bones it took
to keep the tail held
high and straight back.
Opposite page: A
Velociraptor surprises a
chicken-size dinosaur.
The raptor was fast and
smart enough to kill
small, agile prey.

dinosaurs held their tails up off the ground, unlike modern reptiles. It also means that dinosaurs, especially the two-legged meat-eaters, were able to move much more quickly than any large reptile could.

Velociraptor's tail accounted for fully half of the full length of its body. Long, bony rods ran back along the tail to help keep it straight and stiff. The tail kept the animal balanced as it ran. Moving the tail like a rudder from one side to the other probably let *Velociraptor* make sharp turns as it ran without losing speed or balance. Thanks to its tail, *Velociraptor* probably could have turned more quickly than a galloping ostrich.

Velociraptor Packs

Scientists are not sure whether *Velociraptors* hunted in packs, but there's good evidence to think they did. The evidence comes from one of *Velociraptor*'s cousins, *Deinonychus*. *Deinonychus* lived about 20 million years before *Velociraptor*, in what is now Montana. Digging there, scientists found the fossil remains of what appears to have been a *Deinonychus* hunt.

This illustration is based on a fossil find. A pack of *Deinonychus* attacks a medium-sized plant-eater called *Tenontosaurus*.

Three *Deinonychus* fossils were found together. Near them was the fossil of a large plant-eater, called *Tenontosaurus*. It was about 25 feet (8 m) long, and weighed one and a half tons (1.4 t). The *Tenontosaurus* skeleton appears to have been ripped apart. It looks like a *Deinonychus* pack jumped the plant-eater. The *Tenonto-saurus* fought for its life, possibly killing three of the raptors before the rest of the pack overcame it. It's likely that *Velociraptor* also hunted in packs, as it and *Deinonychus* were quite similar animals.

If *Velociraptor* hunted in packs, it may have attacked some of the larger plant-eaters of the time. *Probactrosaurus*, an iguanodontid dinosaur, was about 30 feet (9 m) long and weighed as much as a small elephant. "Duck-billed" dinosaurs also shared *Velociraptor*'s world. They were about the same size and weight as *Iguanodon*. A pack of 10 to 12 *Velociraptors*, using their big brains to work together, could probably have attacked and killed dinosaurs this big.

Velociraptor was an active hunter, but that doesn't mean it would have turned down an easy meal. Not all animals die in combat. Many kinds of accidents can cripple an animal. Once crippled, an animal will not survive for long in the wild. If *Velociraptor* smelled a dying animal, it would have sought it out. It may then have attacked, or waited for the animal to die before moving in for the feast.

A ceratopsian is swarmed over by dromaeosaurs. The young plant-eater will become their next meal.

Dinosaurs with Feathers

Velociraptor and its cousins had many birdlike traits. Their bones were full of air pockets like the bones of modern birds. They had hip bones that look like those of birds. And we know that some dinosaurs related to Velociraptor had feathers. Fossils found recently in China show that some small, meat-eating dinosaurs had feathers that resemble those of modern birds.

So far, five different types of feathered dinosaurs have been uncovered in northwestern China. The soft, fine soil in this area preserved the imprints of the feathers. One of these feathered dinosaurs, Sinornithosaurus, was smaller than Velociraptor, but shared the raptor group's sharp teeth and large killing claws. This means that they were related. It is quite possible that Velociraptor also had feathers of some kind.

Another version of what a feathered Velociraptor might have looked like. Only the head, hands, and lower legs are uncovered.

The feet of Velociraptor resembled the feet of modern birds in that there were four toes on each foot. But Velociraptor's toes all faced forward. The first toes of birds extend backward so they can grip the branches of trees.

One of the largest raptors yet discovered, *Utahraptor* is named for the state where its fossils were found. Here a pair of them are on the hunt for their next victim.

Having feathers does not mean these dinosaurs flew. Like fur on mammals, feathers would have helped keep the dinosaurs warm as nighttime temperatures dropped. When it was hot, the feathers would have shielded their skin from the sun's rays.

New Stories from Old Bones

The discovery of *Velociraptor* and, later, its cousin *Deinonychus*, helped change the way scientists thought about dinosaurs. These small, fast, active hunters gave them a new vision for how dinosaurs must have looked, lived, and acted so many millions of years ago.

The dromaeosaurid family was strong and diversified by the time the Age of Dinosaurs came to a close. Quite suddenly, about 65 million years ago, disaster struck. The dromaeosaurs, along with many other species of animals, became extinct.

Scientists think an asteroid impact caused the end of the Age of Dinosaurs. A giant rock from space hit the earth some 65 million years ago, causing worldwide destruction. At the same time, there were massive volcanic eruptions in Asia. Both would have polluted the air, and may have blocked out sunlight for years. Plants died. Plant-eating dinosaurs died for lack of food. And then so did the predators that fed on them. And the Age of Dinosaurs came to a close, more than 200 million years after it began.

This page and opposite page: Two *Velociraptor* pairs bed down for the night. The pair above sleeps in the undergrowth. The pair opposite has made a bed of leaves and branches.

GLOSSARY

Achillobatos (a-KILL-o-BAH-tose): one of the largest known dromaeosaurs.

ankylosaurs (an-KIE-luh-sawrz): group of plant-eating armored dinosaurs with low, barrel-shaped bodies.

ceratopsian (ser-uh-TOP-see-un): a group of four-legged dinosaurs with short tails, huge heads, and a bony frill covering the neck.

Deinonychus (die-NON-ih-kus): a meat-eating dinosaur with a sharp claw on the second toe of each foot.

dromaeosaurids (DROH-mee-uh-SAWR-idz): a family of small to mid-sized, two-legged meat-eaters.

dromaeosaurs (DROH-mee-uh-sawrz): the group of dinosaurs to which raptors belong.

fossil (FAH-sill): a remnant of a living organism that has turned to stone over time.

hatchling (HACH-ling): any animal just born from an egg.

Iguanodon (ih-GWAN-uh-don): a plant-eating dinosaur with spiky thumbs on its "hands."

iguanodontids (ih-guan-uh-DON-tidz): belonging to the *Iguanodon* family of plant-eating dinosaurs.

maniraptoran (MAN-ih-RAP-tor-an): belonging to the maniraptors, a group of small, active, agile theropods.

Oviraptor (OH-vi-RAP-tor): a meat-eating dinosaur.

Parasaurolophus (PAR-uh-SAWR-uh-LOH-fus): a plant-eating "duck-billed" dinosaur.

prairies (PRER-eez): areas of grassland with few trees.

predator (PRED-uh-tor): an animal that hunts and eats other animals for food.

prey (pray): any animal that is hunted as food.

Probactrosaurus (proh-BAK-tro-SAWR-us): a plant-eating dinosaur.

Protoceratops (PRO-tuh-SER-uh-tops): an ancestor of *Triceratops*.

pterosaurs (TERR-uh-sawrz): flying reptiles from the Mesozoic era.

sauropods (SAWR-uh-podz): a group of four-legged, plant-eating dinosaurs.

Sinornithosaurus (SINE-orn-ith-uh-SAWR-us): similar to the *Velociraptor*, but smaller and partially covered in feathers.

Tenontosaurus (te-NON-tuh-SAWR-us): a large plant-eating dinosaur.

theropods (ther-UH-podz): group of two-legged meat-eaters that had birdlike qualities.

trackways (TRAK-wayz): footprints left in the mud that have changed to stone over a long time.

Triceratops (try-SER-uh-tops): a ceratopsid dinosaur with a three-horned face, powerful beaked jaws, and a short, bony frill.

Tyrannosaurus rex (tie-RAN-uh-SAWR-us REX): a tyrannosaurid. One of the largest meat-eaters that ever lived.

Utahraptor (YOO-tah-RAP-tor): a meat-eating dinosaur with a long, curved claw on each foot.

Velociraptor (veh-LOS-ih-RAP-tor): a dromaeosaurid with birdlike qualities, thought to have been a dangerous predator.

INDEX

Ankylosaurs, 12–13

Asteroid impact, 30

Brains, of dromaeosaurids, 12

China, feathered dinosaurs from, 26

Deinonychus, 8–9, 12–13
behavior of, 30
pack hunting by, 20–24
size of, 8

Dromaeosaurids

extinction of, 30
hunting by, 10–13, 16
Velociraptor grouped with, 10–12

Gobi Desert, *Velociraptor* from, 12

Maniraptoran theropods, feathers on, 10–11

Montana, *Deinonychus* from, 20

Oviraptor, 16

Pack hunting, 20–25
Parasaurolophus, 10
Probactrosaurus, 24
Protoceratops, 10

Sauropods, 10
Sinornithosaurus, 26

Tails, of dinosaurs, 18–20
Tenontosaurus, 22–24
Trackways, 18
Triceratops, 6
Tyrannosaurus rex, 10

Utahraptor, 10, 16, 28–29

Velociraptor
arms of, 14
behavior of, 30–31
and birds, 26
classification of, 10–12
extinction of, 30
eyes of, 16–18
feathers on, 10–11, 26–30
head of, 16–18
hunting by, 12, 14–15
legs of, 14
mammals, as prey of, 7
naming of, 14
pack hunting by, 20–24
plant-eaters, as prey of, 6, 10
as predator, 6–10, 14–18
size of, 6, 8
skeleton of, 20
speed of, 14
tail of, 20
teeth of, 16

www.ingramcontent.com/pod-product-compliance
Lightning Source LLC
Chambersburg PA
CBHW060801150426
42813CB00058B/2785